pretty sparks

emi999

D0832557

snowheel

BinBenny37

spin9010

Prettybethany

Sparrkle

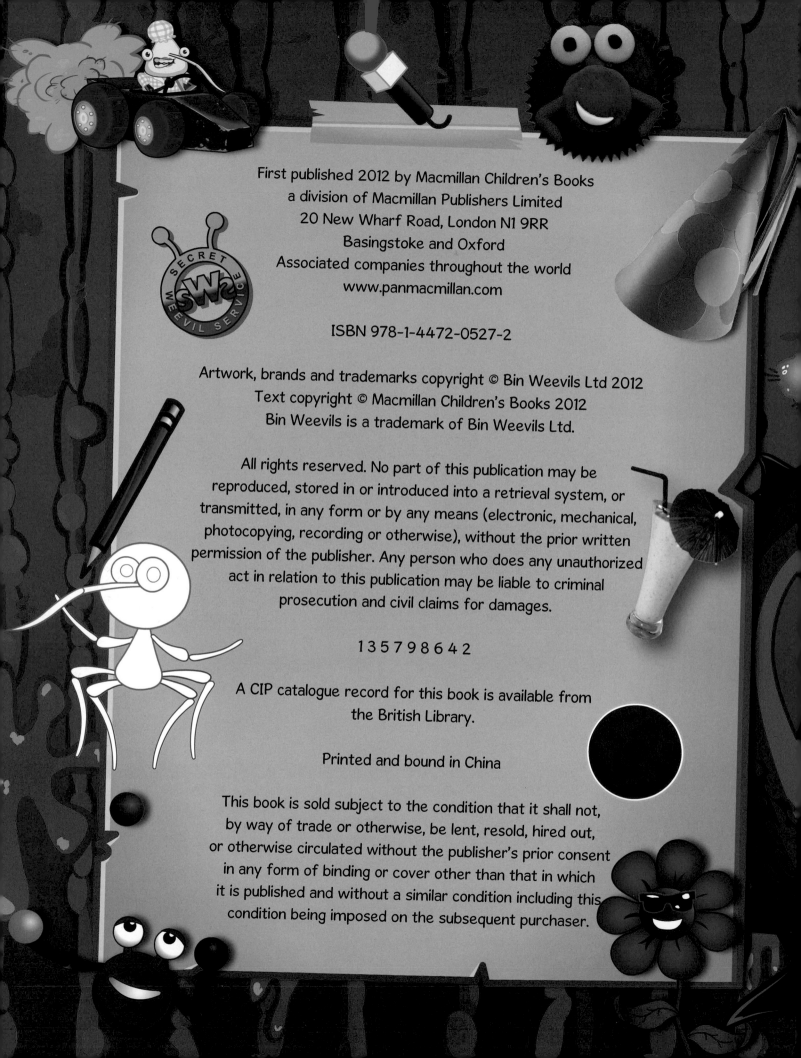

First published 2012 by Macmillan Children's Books
a division of Macmillan Publishers Limited
20 New Wharf Road, London N1 9RR
Basingstoke and Oxford
Associated companies throughout the world
www.panmacmillan.com

ISBN 978-1-4472-0527-2

1 3 5 7 9 8 6 4 2

A CIP catalogue record for this book is available from
the British Library.

Printed and bound in China

THIS BIN WEEVILS ANNUAL BELONGS TO

_____

CONTENTS

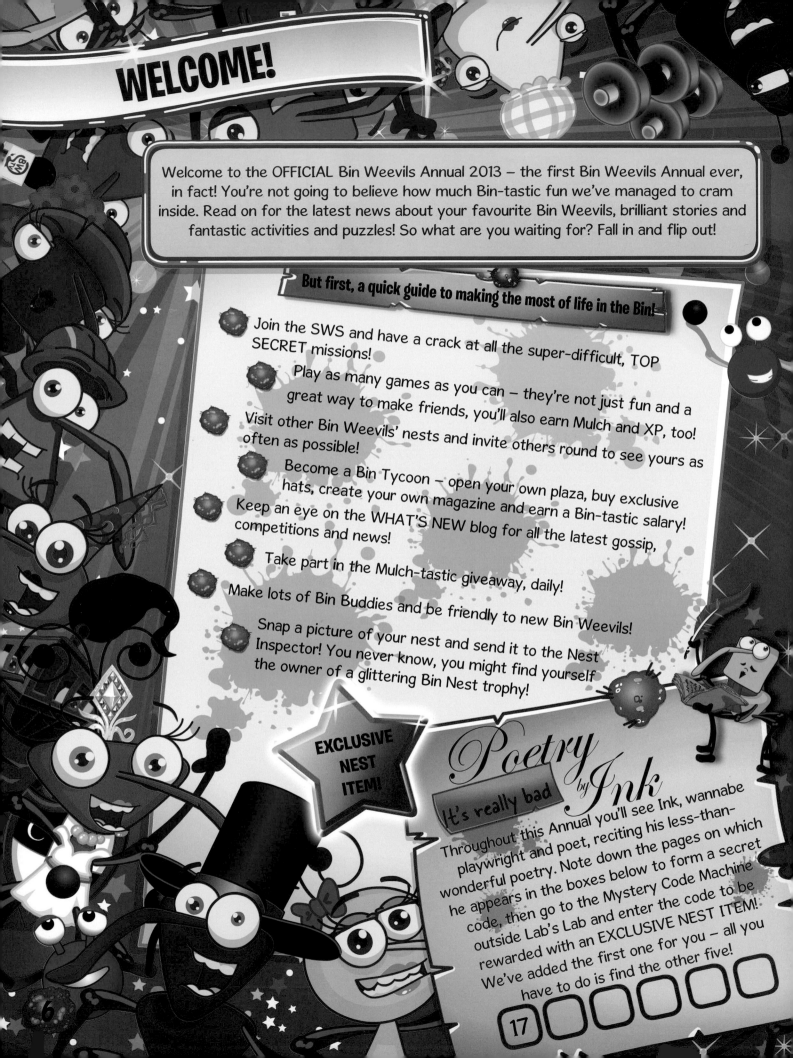

WELCOME!

Welcome to the OFFICIAL Bin Weevils Annual 2013 – the first Bin Weevils Annual ever, in fact! You're not going to believe how much Bin-tastic fun we've managed to cram inside. Read on for the latest news about your favourite Bin Weevils, brilliant stories and fantastic activities and puzzles! So what are you waiting for? Fall in and flip out!

But first, a quick guide to making the most of life in the Bin!

- Join the SWS and have a crack at all the super-difficult, TOP SECRET missions!

- Play as many games as you can – they're not just fun and a great way to make friends, you'll also earn Mulch and XP, too!

- Visit other Bin Weevils' nests and invite others round to see yours as often as possible!

- Become a Bin Tycoon – open your own plaza, buy exclusive hats, create your own magazine and earn a Bin-tastic salary!

- Keep an eye on the WHAT'S NEW blog for all the latest gossip, competitions and news!

- Take part in the Mulch-tastic giveaway, daily!

- Make lots of Bin Buddies and be friendly to new Bin Weevils!

- Snap a picture of your nest and send it to the Nest Inspector! You never know, you might find yourself the owner of a glittering Bin Nest trophy!

EXCLUSIVE NEST ITEM!

Poetry by Ink

It's really bad

Throughout this Annual you'll see Ink, wannabe playwright and poet, reciting his less-than-wonderful poetry. Note down the pages on which he appears in the boxes below to form a secret code, then go to the Mystery Code Machine outside Lab's Lab and enter the code to be rewarded with an EXCLUSIVE NEST ITEM! We've added the first one for you – all you have to do is find the other five!

17 ☐ ☐ ☐ ☐ ☐

The start of a new year is the perfect time to set yourself some weevily goals! Writing them down in your Annual will help you focus on them (and, hopefully, keep them!). Last year, Clott set himself a goal to cut down on his six-a-day Bin Burger habit, but he only lasted until January the second. Let's hope he does better this year!

Make a note of the things you want to achieve in the space below. At the end of the year, colour in a star next to each goal you manage to keep. No cheating – be honest! There's some space at the bottom for you to write down your own goal idea.

MY WEEVILY GOALS ARE:

⭐ To complete this mission: _____

⭐ To achieve this time in Weevil Wheels: _____

⭐ To achieve this nest score: _____

To buy this hat:
(draw pic here)

⭐ To meet this famous Bin Weevil: _____

⭐ To reach level ____

To earn this trophy:
(draw pic here)

To own this nest item:
(draw pic here)

My goal idea: _____

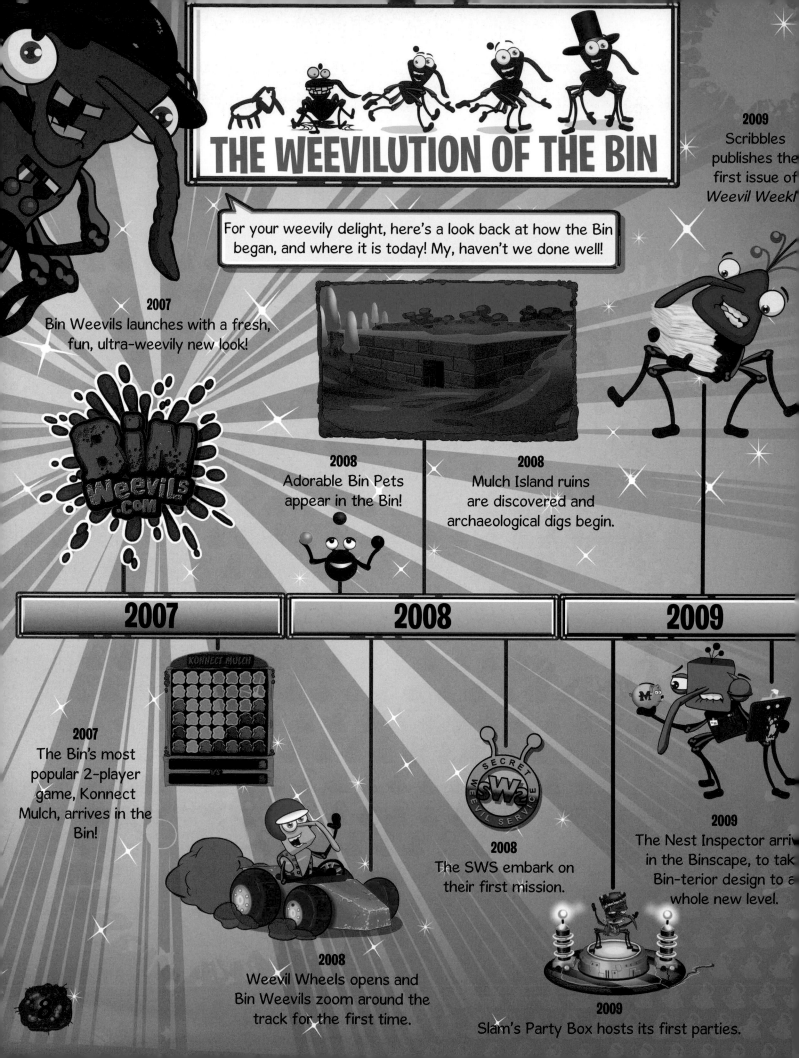

THE WEEVILUTION OF THE BIN

For your weevily delight, here's a look back at how the Bin began, and where it is today! My, haven't we done well!

2009
Scribbles publishes the first issue of *Weevil Week...*

2007
Bin Weevils launches with a fresh, fun, ultra-weevily new look!

2008
Adorable Bin Pets appear in the Bin!

2008
Mulch Island ruins are discovered and archaeological digs begin.

2007 2008 2009

2007
The Bin's most popular 2-player game, Konnect Mulch, arrives in the Bin!

2008
The SWS embark on their first mission.

2009
The Nest Inspector arri... in the Binscape, to tak... Bin-terior design to a whole new level.

2008
Weevil Wheels opens and Bin Weevils zoom around the track for the first time.

2009
Slam's Party Box hosts its first parties.

2010
Dosh opens Uncle Slosh's Bin Weevil Changer machine to the weevily public!

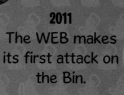
CHANGE THE WAY YOUR BIN WEEVIL LOOKS HERE!

BIN WEEVIL CHANGER

2011
Scribbles hosts the biggest ever nest party to celebrate his one hundredth issue of *Weevil Weekly*.

100TH ISSUE OF WEEVIL WEEKLY

2012
New level trophies and new levels are released!

2011
The WEB makes its first attack on the Bin.

2012
Dosh announces his brand new currency.

2011
Tink's Tree reaches full size, begins to blossom and releases seeds for the very first time.

2010
:h Bin Weevil's nest is allocated ts very own lush Bin Garden.

2010

2011

2012

2010
lem's Hat Shop opens to ovide style-conscious Bin eevils with hip headgear.

2011
Lab's Mystery Code Machine is built.

2012
Bin Weevils are given the opportunity to make their own racetracks with the Weevily Track Builder!

2012
Bin Bots arrive in the Bin!

HAGGLE HUT

2011
Castle Gam's SWS Headquarters gets a hi-tech makeover.

What does the future hold? Watch this space to find out . . .

2010
The Haggle Hut opens its doors for business.

THE BEST OF THE BEST

As the Bin's resident reporter, I've been taking weevily polls all year to discover which items, places and events are really wowing you. So for the first time in Bin history I'm delighted to release these FASCINATING poll findings!

Most Wanted Nest Items

Secret Tree

Whale Sofa

Mini Dosh's Palace

Elephant Wall Ornament

Scribbles Bed

Lab's Craziest Inventions

Black Hole In A Box

Lab's Invisibility Potion

Venus Flytrap Wrangler

Shake-you-awake Alarm Clock

I recently managed to grab a scintillating five-minute interview with Dosh, the Bin's most minted Bin Weevil, and I gained some very interesting insight into what makes him tick. (Aside from the obvious – Mulch!)

SCRIBBLES
Asks
DOSH

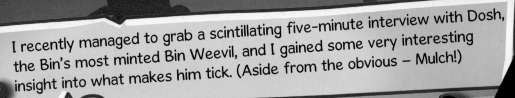

Crown or Top Hat?
A nice top hat never goes out of style!

Mulch Island or Tycoon Island?
Well, Tycoon Island has that A-M-A-Z-I-N-G statue of me, so there's really no contest, is there?

Figg's Cafe or Tum's Diner?
Figg's Cafe is best for a spot of afternoon tea. (Sorry, Tum!)

Konnect Mulch or Flip Mulch?
Mulch, Mulch, Mulch! I like them both, but if I had to pick it would be Konnect Mulch, because I always beat Posh at that one!

Flowers or Mushrooms?
Hmmm, tricky. Both flowers and mushrooms can be harvested for Mulch, but I prefer flowers because they make my Palace smell nice and fresh.

Nest Party or Nightclub?
Oh, definitely nightclub! The more Bin Weevils, the better!

Tink's Blocks or Weevil Wheels?
Weevil Wheels. My great-grandfather left me some retro race cars that I've been meaning to test out on the tracks!

Spending or Saving?
A little bit of both, I suppose. I just love to shop, but I also love rolling in all my lovely Mulch!

Trophies or Collectibles?
Trophies can make any nest look bling-tastic! My favourite trophies are the glittering ones that are overflowing with diamonds and Mulch!

Flum's Fountain or Tink's Tree?
Flum's Fountain. Tink's Tree is great for green-fingered gardeners, but I like instant Mulch myself!

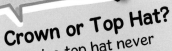

HOW TO DRAW DOSH

Study this picture of me very carefully, then copy it into the grid below, using the squares to guide you. Finish my portrait with a flourish of colour, then stand back and admire your masterpiece!

Do you want to hear the story about Scribbles' blunt pencil?

No, it's pointless.

HEM'S STYLE Q&A

Darlings! Hem here, owner of Hem's Hats and style adviser to the stars. But I'm sure you knew that already. I'm only too delighted to be able to share my hottest tips on how to wear the hippest headwear in the Bin. I get so many messages from style-conscious Bin Weevils that I decided to address the most common concerns in my first ever Style Q&A session! Enjoy, darlings!

Q Dear Hem, my friend insists on wearing the same old baseball cap day in, day out. I need a really fab hat to tempt him out of it! Any ideas? Sincerely, Weevily Style Queen.

A Dear Weevily Style Queen, it certainly sounds like your friend could do with freshening up his headgear – can he be persuaded to try a Cowboy Hat, for a boyish yet stylish look? Love, Hem.

Q Dear Hem, nothing seems to go with my square head. Can you help me find the perfect hat? Thank you, Mr Right Angles.

A Dear Mr Right Angles, I can sympathize! I find a nice, soft, round-edged hat perfectly complements my angular face. Try a Bucket Hat or a Cupcake Hat. Love, Hem.

Q Dear Hem, my friend is having a birthday party at her Tycoon Plaza on Saturday. What kind of hat should I wear to make sure I stand out from the crowds? Yours, Loves To Stand Out.

A Dear Loves To Stand Out, try the Bling Top Hat. It'll catch those disco lights like nothing else! Love, Hem.

Q Dear Hem, I've always been a crown guy, but recently I've been feeling the urge to change my look. What would you recommend for a super-sophisticated Bin Weevil such as myself? Sincerely, Upper-Crust Urwin.

A Dear Upper-Crust Urwin, a Bin Weevil after Dosh's own heart! Have you considered a Classic Top Hat? Or perhaps a Bowler Hat for a classic gentleman's look? Love, Hem.

Q Dear Hem, I need a cosy hat for those chilly winter months. What would you recommend to keep my antennae warm? Thanks, Shivering Antennae.

A Dear Shivering Antennae, my Fluffy Hat is perfect for a cold winter's day, and stylish, too. Stay snug! Hem.

I'm always keen to look at new and original hat designs. Why not give hat design a go yourself? Draw your ideal hat here!

These five beauties are my bestselling hats. Darling, you simply MUST own at least one of these!

TRICORNE HAT

JESTER'S HAT

ROSE HAT

INDIAN HEADDRESS

BASEBALL CAP

Each hat appears one more time throughout this book. Can you spot them all? Write down the page on which you find each hat in the box provided, then go to the Mystery Code Machine outside Lab's Lab and enter the code, to claim a mystery reward! Don't forget, this page doesn't count!

HOW TO DRAW BUNTY

Follow these simple steps to draw a lovely picture of me!

1. Draw a circle (for the head) overlapping a triangle (for the body). **TOP TIP: It's best to use a pencil and draw lightly at first, in case you make a mistake.**

2. Draw a light dotted line down, and another across, the middle of the head – this will help you to position the eyes and nose. You can rub these out later. Next, draw two circles for the eyes and two thin sausage shapes for the nose.

3. For the arms and legs, draw some more sausage shapes – one short and fat, one long and thin.

4. Draw a squashed circle for a hand, then add a sausage shape for the thumb. Do the same for the opposite hand, then draw an outline around the shapes.

5. Add some squashed circles for the elbows and the knees, then draw in the feet.

6. For the skirt, draw a rectangle, then add some wave shapes.

7. Draw in Bunty's mouth, antenna, eyelashes and bow. To finish, draw over your pencil lines in the colour of your choice. Fabulous!

BUNTY'S FAVOURITE THINGS

Bunty is the Bin's gossip queen – she always knows what's going on! She works in the Tycoon Shop on Tycoon Island, selling fancy gadgets to Tycoons, so she hears lots of interesting gossip during the day! She's also an avid celebrity spotter and spends her spare time hunting down autographs at celeb parties. These are her absolute favourite things to do in the Bin!

V.I.P. Pass

ACCESS ALL AREAS

Having a girls' day out at the Smoothie Shack with her besties.

SMOOTHIE

Snagging a backstage pass to a hot Bin event.

Poetry by *Ink*

It's really bad

Ode to Cheese
Cheese, cheese, delicious cheese,
Could I have some cheese on my sandwich, please?
Cheese with holes, cheese with mould,
Great cheesy stories must be told.

WEEVIL WEEKLY

Reading *Weevil Weekly* to catch up with the latest news.

Being the first to hear an absolutely Bin-tastic piece of gossip!

Getting her photo snapped with a celeb!

Bunty,
ve Big Weevil

GAM AND HIS PET DRAGON

SCRIBBLES
Asks
GAM

Gam is the oldest Bin Weevil in the Bin, and there's no end to the cool things I've discovered about him! One of the strangest is that he hasn't got a regular Bin Pet like the rest of us . . . Oh, no! Instead, he's the proud owner of a whopping great DRAGON! I thought I'd pop in for a visit and fire some questions at Gam! (Geddit? *Fire* some questions?)

What's your pet dragon's name?
Colin! I named him after my great-great-grandfather, Gam Colin IV.

What do you feed him?
He loves to eat the beans harvested from the giant beanstalk. The best beans come from the very top of the stalk. Sometimes I have to climb all the way up and into the sky to harvest them. Flying would be faster than climbing, but (would you believe it) Colin is afraid of heights!

How do you make sure Colin stays fit and healthy?
He spends a lot of time marauding around the tunnels under the castle. Sometimes I don't see him for days at a time, whic makes me wonder whether he's got himself lost . . . but he always finds his way back eventually. And he's usually picked up something very interesting on his journeys.

What has Colin found in the tunnels latel
Just the other day, he came back with an old map th revealed several secret underground passageways Someone must have hidden it in the tunnels a long time ago. No doubt it'll prove very useful to the SW

Hmm . . . what a mysterious egg!

Awww, isn't he cute?

Colin's First Birthday!

COLIN FACT FILE

Colin weighs as much as 18,215 Bin Pets and is as big as eleven nests!

The egg that Colin hatched from was rainbow-coloured – which is very rare for a dragon's egg.

Colin wants to learn to play an instrument, but nobody has made a guitar big enough yet!

He likes exploring, being sung to and having his ears scratched.

He dislikes heights, loud noises and brushing his teeth.

He can fry breakfast with his own breath.

Best Friends

Home Sweet Home

11 × ⬅ = Colin

Brushing Teeth

23

DRAGON PUZZLES

Colin the dragon just LOVES wordsearches. You wouldn't think a dragon could find time for wo
puzzles in his busy schedule of breathing fire and guarding the castle, but Colin does! So I've
created this special dragon-themed wordsearch in his honour. Be warned – it's SUPER-
DIFFICULT, and only the most observant Bin Weevils will succeed in finding all the hidden wor

```
E R T Y Y H T E E T O A S O F
B G H G B P L K A F D S A F I
U I G H F D T I Z X V V I T P
K L I O O E L I T P E R O H I
H E R I F P T E M L E H H I V
F R B N H N M E R F I U H U Y
A A R F D I O N I A O G S M Y
B R U B U H J G A D R G U R S
S E O L N B H N A R I E R G F
B P A A G T I S L R D N B G Y
M A G H E L I E C U D H H K N
G P V R O E L T S A C H T M O
I L I C N B G D S S L M O M R
O L F R I E N D L Y I Y O U E
G A H R E H S I U G N I T X E
T W Y U W I N G S X P L P M N
```

FIRE ☐

SCALY ☐

TEETH ☐

TAIL ☐

HOT ☐

CASTLE ☐

RUG ☐

GAM☐

COLIN

EGG☐

WINGS ☐

REPTILE

TOOTHBRUSH ☐   EXTINGUISHER ☐   ☐   DRAG ☐

HEL☐   ☐   ☐   ☐   ☐   DUNGEON ☐

TOOTHBRUSH PUZZLE

Gam has sent Clott out to buy Colin a new toothbrush, but while he was browsing he knocked the toothbrushes all over the floor! All the price tags have come off and the shop owner can't remember how much they are. Using these clues, can you match the correct price tag to the correct toothbrush? Draw lines to match them up.

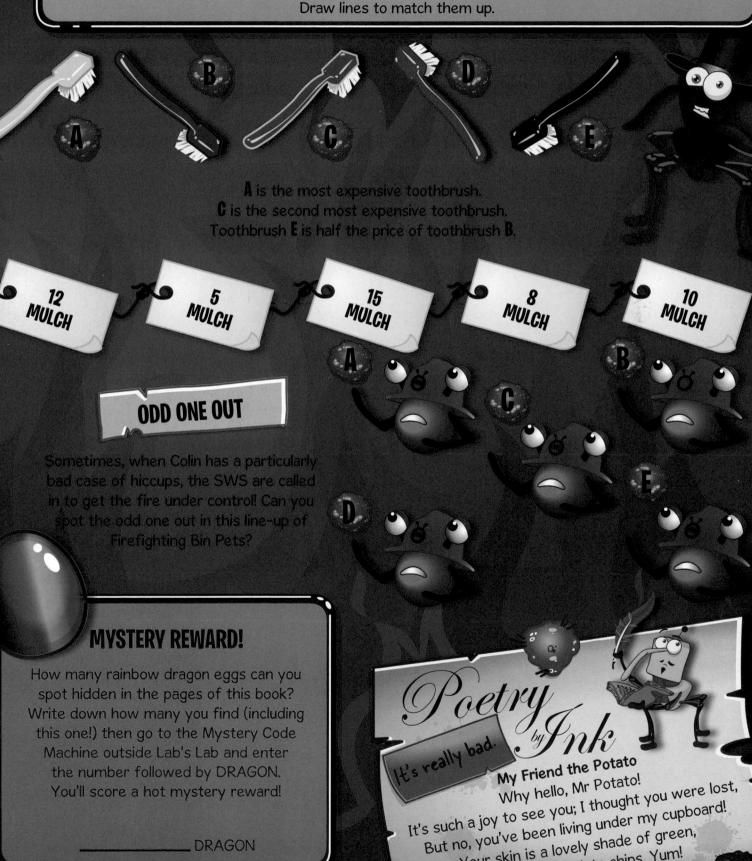

A is the most expensive toothbrush.
C is the second most expensive toothbrush.
Toothbrush **E** is half the price of toothbrush **B**.

12 MULCH   5 MULCH   15 MULCH   8 MULCH   10 MULCH

ODD ONE OUT

Sometimes, when Colin has a particularly bad case of hiccups, the SWS are called in to get the fire under control! Can you spot the odd one out in this line-up of Firefighting Bin Pets?

MYSTERY REWARD!

How many rainbow dragon eggs can you spot hidden in the pages of this book? Write down how many you find (including this one!) then go to the Mystery Code Machine outside Lab's Lab and enter the number followed by DRAGON. You'll score a hot mystery reward!

_____ DRAGON

Poetry by Ink

It's really bad.

My Friend the Potato
Why hello, Mr Potato!
It's such a joy to see you; I thought you were lost,
But no, you've been living under my cupboard!
Your skin is a lovely shade of green,
I will make you into chips. Yum!

CELEBRITY SNAPS

I've been snapping pics of the Bin's coolest celebs all day, but I've zoomed in too far on some of my pictures! Can you work out which famous Bin Weevil each body part belongs to? Draw lines to match each picture to the correct Bin Weevil name.

1

2

3

4

5

6

Figg

Bing

The Nest Inspector

Bunty

Gam

Gong

SPECIAL OPS TRAINING

TOP SECRET

TINK

SWS Agent. Tends to struggle with missions. Brilliant chap, but he's usually too busy helping Clott out of mischief to be much use.

TOP SECRET

Gam

Me! Leader of the SWS, retired superhero and oldest Bin Weevil in the Bin!

Welcome to the Secret Weevil Service Agent Training Room! Let me introduce you to the fearless Bin Weevils who head up the SWS!

If you want to be a member of this elite organization of problem-solving, crime-fighting Bin Weevils (and Tink and Clott), you'll need to prove you've got what it takes. If you manage to complete the following tests, you can consider yourself an SWS Agent of the highest level. Good luck, Agent!

SKILL: BIN KNOWLEDGE

Your Bin knowledge plays a key role in how well you perform as an SWS Agent. Take this true or false quiz to test yourself!

T   F

1. Tink and Clott are cousins.   ☐ ☐

2. Gong runs the Haggle Hut at Gong's Pipenest.   ☐ ☐

3. Tum's Diner has a jukebox.   ☐ ☐

4. Octeelia is Gam's oldest friend.   ☐ ☐

TOP SECRET

CLOTT

SWS Agent and friend of Tink. Tends to struggle A LOT with missions. Brilliant chap, but unfortunately has the attention span of a Dirt Doughnut.

TRIGG

Knows all there is to know about Secret Weevil Service equipment. Expert on everything in the SWS armoury.

TOP SECRET

KONG FU

From martial arts to marksmanship, Kong's the expert on everything an SWS agent needs to know. He's in charge of training all new recruits!

BUNTY

TOP SECRET

Top SWS Agent. Great to have around in a crisis and an invaluable source of Bin knowledge thanks to all that gossiping she does on her days off.

SKILL: LOGIC

Having the ability to think logically is essential for being able to figure out mysteries. Try these Sudoku squares to boost your logic power. Each row across and down should contain the numbers 1-4 only once.

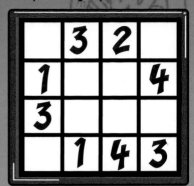

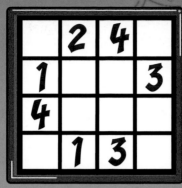

SKILL: OBSERVATION

An SWS Agent's observation skills must be second-to-none. Test yourself with these puzzles.

ODD ONE OUT

Can you spot the odd one out in each row?

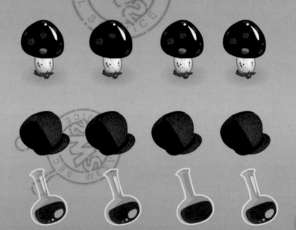

COMPLETE THE SEQUENCE

Can you spot the pattern in each row below, then finish the sequence by drawing the next item in the box provided?

SKILL: PHYSICAL FITNESS

SWS Agents need to be super-fit, like Gong, so they can dash around after criminals. Test your fitness level by creating an obstacle course for you and your friends to complete. Here are some ideas to get you started:

- Ask an adult if you can have an old sheet to tunnel under.
- Set up a slalom course using stuffed toys and weave in and out of them.
- Set up hurdles to jump over, using old towels.
- Set up hula hoops in a row and jump from one hoop to the next.
- Throw beanbags into a washing basket.

If you're feeling particularly competitive, you could time yourself against your friends. The winner is the person who completes the obstacle course in the shortest time.

GONG'S TOP TIP

Finish your obstacle course with ten star jumps!

CRACK THE CODE

Pssst! Come in, Agent. I've intercepted a coded message sent by Weevil X to Octeelia, and I think I've managed to crack the code! Using my notes, can you translate the message? Must dash, someone's got to take Colin for walkies . . .

TOP SECRET

4,22

8,7,9,18,16,22

24,26,8,7,15,22

20,26,14

7,12,13,18,20,19,7!

TOP SECRET

A=26 B=25 C=24 D=23 E=22 F=21 G=20 H=19 I=18 J=17 K=16 L=15 M=14

N=13 O=12 P=11 Q=10 R=9 S=8 T=7 U=6 V=5 W=4 X=3 Y=2 Z=1

_____ _____ / _____ _____

_____ / _____ _____

_____ / _____ _____ _____ _____ _____ _____ _____

Poetry by Ink

It's really bad

Gam
Gam.
Gam likes jam,
And ham,
But not together.
Gam.

Queen of the camera Snappy has spotted some suspicious behaviour outside Dosh's Palace, and snapped a snappy photo to show the SWS. But something seems to have gone wrong with the copy. Can you spot ten differences between the original picture and the copy?

ORIGINAL

COPY

Match the letter for each item to the correct Bin Weevil girl using the boxes below. Each girl has five items.

A. Propeller Key Ring

B. Jewels

C. Oil Can

D. Bin Pet Bowl

E. Map

F. Spare Flying Goggles

G. Spanner

H. Make-up

I. Bin Pet Treats

J. Heart Charm Key Ring

Mulch

Poetry by Ink

It's really bad.

My Zesty Orange Peel
I loved my zesty Orange Peel,
How I was besotted!
But imagine how it made me feel,
When I learned it had been Clotted!

THE BIN WEEVILS SONG

Now you can sing along with us when we sing the Bin Weevils Song, which is often and with gusto.

FALL IN, FLIP OUT!

All together now!

Chorus
Weeviling about
Fall in, flip out!
Weeviling about
BIN WEEVILS!

Verse
Jump up, step down
Weevil shake
Stomp your feet round
Through the Binscape!
Hands up, shout out
Push the ceiling
Shake your hair out
We're Bin Weeviling!

Rap
Play games all day, to do up our nest
We live in the Bin, cos the Bin's the best!
We live for Mulch, so we can be
The best Bin Weevils you'll ever see!

TYCOON HATS

Feeling crafty? Learn how to make some of the coolest hats in the Bin!

HOW TO MAKE: Zing's Hat

THE ULTIMATE PARTY HAT!

YOU WILL NEED:
- A large piece of thin purple card that will fit around your head
- A pencil
- Scissors
- Sticky tape
- A stapler
- Coloured paper – yellow, green and pink
- A glue stick
- Crepe paper – yellow, green and pink
- Some thin elastic (optional)

Younger Bin Weevils will need an adult to help with cutting/stapling.

1. Roughly draw the largest semicircle you can on your large piece of thin purple card and cut it out.

2. Pinch the middle of the straight edge into a little point, then bring the two corners of the curved edge together.

3. Ask an adult or friend to hold the hat on your head so you can check how tightly you will need to tape or staple the two edges together. Ask them to tape the edges together securely while the hat is still on your head, or take it off and staple it.

4. Secure the hat with even more tape on the inside. (We don't want it popping open!)

5. Cut lots of circles of different sizes out of your coloured paper. Stick these on to your hat with your glue stick.

6. Cut two long strips of each colour of crepe paper. Tape these to the top of your hat.

7. Make a hole on either side of the bottom of the hat. Thread one end of your thin elastic through one hole and tie a knot in the end of it so it won't pop all the way out.

8. Put the hat back on your head and thread the elastic under your chin, then thread the end through your second hole.

9. Secure the elastic with another knot so that it is tight enough to keep the hat on your head. But not too tight!

10. If you prefer, you can clip your hat to your head using hair grips.

And you're done! You look ama-ZING!

YOU WILL NEED:
- A large piece of silver card
- Scissors
- A pencil
- A ruler
- Sticky tape
- A stapler
- A small piece of red card

Younger Bin Weevils will need an adult to help with cutting/stapling.

HOW TO MAKE:
Diamond Crown With Rubies

FOR TRUE BIN ROYALTY!

Well hello, Your Highness!

1. Cut a piece of silver card that fits exactly round your head, so that it will sit just above your ears. It should be taller than it is wide.

2. Turn the card over, and draw a line horizontally across the card, 10cm from the bottom.

3. On top of the line, you will need to create six equally spaced triangles. You can draw these roughly, or if you want to be accurate, measure the card and divide it exactly into six triangles.

4. Cut along your pencil line so you are left with a row of points on top of a base rectangle.

5. Hold the card round your head, and ask an adult or friend to tape or staple it in place. Take the crown off and tape the inside too.

6. Cut eight squares from your red card and glue one to the top of each point so that they look like diamonds.

7. Pop your crown on your head!

HOW TO MAKE A BIN PET!

I JUST LOVE BIN PETS! AREN'T THEY CUTE!

Hi, I'm Dott! When I'm not in the Bin Pet Shop, I have lots of fun creating Bin Pet models from all sorts of bits and bobs I find lying around! Fancy having a go yourself? I'll show you how to make the best Bin Pet!

YOU WILL NEED:

- Kitchen foil
- Coloured tissue paper
- PVA glue
- A paintbrush
- Scissors
- A pencil
- A ruler
- Coloured pipe cleaners
- Sticky tape
- A 1p coin
- A sheet of thick white paper
- Coloured pens

HOW TO MAKE A BIN PET

1. Cut yourself a large piece of kitchen foil and scrunch it up into a nice round ball, to make the base of your Bin Pet body. This should be about the size of a satsuma.

2. Cut two lengths of pipe cleaner, each four inches long, to make your Bin Pet arms.

3. Tape the arms on to the body by folding a small section so it lies flat against the foil, then cover the ball with another layer of kitchen foil to cover the tape.

4. Cut or tear your tissue paper into small squares.

5. Paint white glue all over the foil ball, then carefully stick the tissue paper squares all over it, until the foil is completely covered.

6. Leave to dry.

TOP TIP

Wear an apron while making your Bin Pet to protect your clothes, and ask an adult to cover the table you will be using with an old sheet or tablecloth.

7. Take a 1p coin and draw round it twice on thick white paper. Cut the circles out to make eyes. Draw black circles in the middle for the pupils, and add a thin crescent of colour to the top of the circle for the eyelids.

8. Cut a small crescent shape from your white paper for the mouth. Stick it in the centre of your Bin Pet's face.

9. Cut two more lengths of pipe cleaner, each 1.5 inches long.

10. Tape these to the top of your Bin Pet by folding a small section so it lies flat against the foil, then cover with squares of tissue paper to hide the tape.

11. Tape your eyes on to the tops of the short lengths of pipe cleaner.

12. Ta-daa! Your very own Bin Pet model!

Mr Trashface

Ms Trashface

Don't forget to take a picture of your model and send it in to pics@binweevils.com! You might see your creation up on the FAN ART section of the WHAT'S NEW blog!

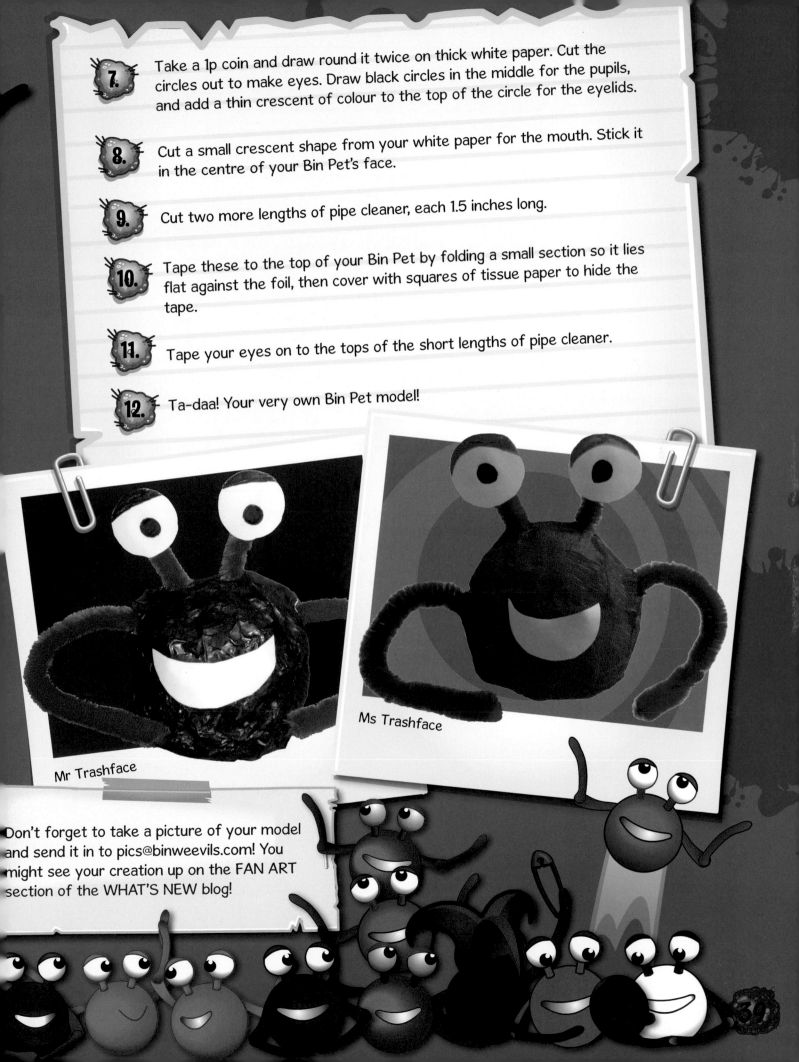

SUPER
SMOOTHIES

Hi, I'm Sip! I just love a nice fruity smoothie at the Smoothie Shack, especially if it's served with a side order of gossip!

Here are some splendid smoothie recipes to try at home. You'll need a blender, a chopping board, a knife and a glass.

Younger Bin Weevils will need to ask an adult to help with chopping and blending.

Each recipe serves one person.

INGREDIENTS:
- One banana
- 150g strawberries, hulled
- 120ml plain yogurt
- 60ml milk

PINK LADY
HOW TO MAKE:

1. Chop your bananas into bite-sized chunks.

2. Chop your strawberries in half.

3. Put all your ingredients in a blender, and blend until smooth.

4. Pour into a glass, and serve!

INGREDIENTS:

- One mango
- The pulp from two passion fruits
- 120ml plain yogurt
- 120ml milk

TROPICAL TREAT
HOW TO MAKE:

1. Peel and stone your mango, then cut into chunks.

2. Cut your passion fruits in half and remove the pulp.

3. Put all your ingredients in a blender, and blend until smooth.

4. Pour into a glass, and serve!

INGREDIENTS:

- 100g honeydew melon chunks
- 2 kiwi fruits
- 120ml plain yogurt
- 60ml millk

SLIME SMOOTHIE
HOW TO MAKE:

1. Peel your kiwi fruit and chop into bite-sized pieces.

2. Put all your ingredients in a blender, and blend until smooth.

3. Pour into a glass, and serve!

TOP TIP

Pop a straw and a paper umbrella into your finished drink to create a truly tropical treat!

BiN PET CUPCAKES

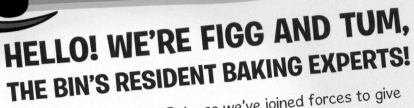

HELLO! WE'RE FIGG AND TUM,
THE BIN'S RESIDENT BAKING EXPERTS!

We both LOVE our Bin Pets, so we've joined forces to give our weevily friends the ultimate Bin Pet Cupcake masterclass!

These sweet treats aren't just yummy, they look super-cute too. They're guaranteed to impress your friends – why not make them for a birthday party or sleepover?

Wear an apron while making these cupcakes, to protect your clothes. Younger Bin Weevils will need to ask an adult to help.

INGREDIENTS FOR 12 CAKES:

- Plain cupcakes in cases, ready to decorate
- 200g icing sugar
- 60ml/4tbsp water
- Food colouring – various colours
- Ready-to-roll icing – various colours
- White chocolate buttons OR white marshmallows
- Writing icing – black and white

EQUIPMENT:
- Mixing bowl
- Wooden spoon
- Dessert spoon
- Sieve
- Mini cookie cutter
- Knife

TOP TIP
Feeling especially creative? Display your Bin Pet cupcake on a plate and surround it with small round sweets so that it looks like it's juggling!

HOW TO MAKE BIN PET CUPCAKES

1. Sieve your icing sugar into a bowl, then add your water and stir until it forms a thick cream. This is your glacé icing.

2. Carefully add a few drops of food colouring at a time to the icing, until it reaches your desired colour.

3. Spread the glacé icing on to the top of your first cupcake using your spoon so that it is completely covered.

4. Roll out a small piece of ready-to-roll icing, and cut a small circle using a mini cookie cutter. Place this in the centre of your cupcake.

5. Draw a small dot of black writing icing into the middle of two white chocolate buttons to make the eyes. You can use white marshmallows instead of buttons if you prefer. Place the eyes on top of your glacé icing.

6. You might also want to add a small crescent of icing on to the top of the eyes, for eyelids.

7. Draw a white smile on to your Bin Pet's face using white writing icing, or take some ready-to-roll white icing and cut a small crescent from it.

8. Make two small sausage shapes from your ready-to-roll icing, and bend them about a third of the way down. Stick these to the sides of the body.

TOP TIP
If your ready-to-roll icing won't stick to your glacé icing, use writing icing to glue it in place.

BIN PETS

They're cool, they're cuddly, they're bouncy, they're barmy . . . they're Bin Pets!

QUESTION #1 FROM THE BOOK OF MOST-ASKED BIN PET QUESTIONS: HOW DO I GET MY BIN PET TO JUMP ON TO MY BACK?

It will take time to train your Bin Pet to jump up on your back, but a little patience is all you need! Here's a step-by-step walkthrough:

Mister Snuggles, yoo-hoo!

1. First, make sure your pet is looking at you – calling your pet's name is a good way to start.

2. Then, stand in front of your pet and jump up and down a few times until your pet begins to imitate you.

3. Once your pet has followed your lead a few times, it will learn the 'Jump On' move, and you will see a new button appear in the pet's action menu. If you click on this button, your Bin Weevil will call for your pet to 'Jump On' and the pet should hop up on to your back! The more times you do this, the faster your pet will respond to the command. A really well-trained pet might even hop on without being called, because it's just so eager to get outside and play!

Once your pet learns to jump on to your back, it can come with you when you leave your nest and share in all your weevily adventures throughout the Bin!

WHAT'S YOUR BIN PET'S PERSONALITY TYPE?

Bin Pets come in all different colours, and they've got a rainbow of personalities too! Take this quiz to find out your pet's personality type.

When your pet wakes up, what's the first thing he/she does?

A. Comes over to you for a pat.
B. Runs around in circles.
C. Wants to go outside.

2 What's your pet's name?

A. Something sweet, like Cutie or Fluffy.
B. Something fierce, like Lightning or Tiger.
C. Something quirky, like Zoodles or Wonko.

3 Does your pet like to do tricks?

A. Sometimes, but I have to give him/her lots of love first!
B. My pet just can't wait to learn new tricks every day!
C. He/she knows some tricks, but doesn't tend to cooperate!

When you take your pet out in the Bin to play, what does he/she do?

A. Sticks close to me and stays on my back most of the time.
B. Rushes eagerly off to play with other Bin Pets.
C. Disappears! I never know where he/she has run off to!

4 If your pet could talk, what do you think he/she would say?

A. You're the best! Now, can I have some cuddles?
B. Hurry up, I want to play! Throw the ball again!
C. Time to go home already? But I was still exploring!

Your Bin Pet
(Draw a picture of your Bin Pet here)

Name: ....
Best trick: ....
Likes: ....
Dislikes: ....
XP gained: ....

MOSTLY As
CUTE AND CUDDLY

Your pet demands loads of love and attention, but is super-sweet and well-behaved. The two of you are absolutely inseparable – awww!

MOSTLY Bs
SPORTY AND ACTIVE

Your pet is always on the go! Whether it's a game of fetch or a spinning trick, showing off a new skill is just so much fun!

MOSTLY Cs
CURIOUS AND MISCHIEVOUS

Your pet can be a little peculiar and hard to keep track of. Mysterious and clever, he/she could totally be a secret agent!

Poetry by Ink

It's really bad.

The Missing Wellies

O, wherefore art thou, my lost wellington boots?
It is muddy outside, I do fear going oot!
Oot? I mean out! Oh bother, that doesn't rhyme.
I'll just carry on writing, I'm sure it's just fine.
I looked under my bed, in the fridge, on the stairs,
Yet I found no sign that my boots had been there!
But then, by the time this fine verse was complete . . .
Good grief! I noticed my boots on my feet.

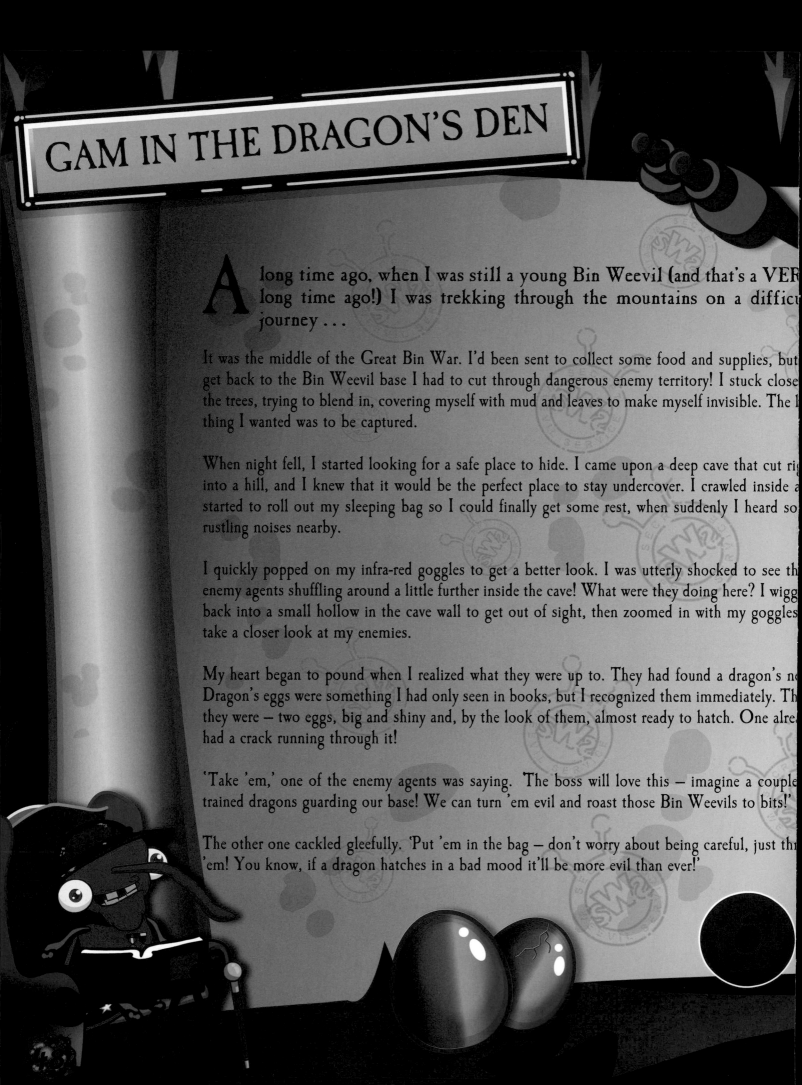

GAM IN THE DRAGON'S DEN

A long time ago, when I was still a young Bin Weevil (and that's a VER long time ago!) I was trekking through the mountains on a difficu journey ...

It was the middle of the Great Bin War. I'd been sent to collect some food and supplies, but get back to the Bin Weevil base I had to cut through dangerous enemy territory! I stuck close the trees, trying to blend in, covering myself with mud and leaves to make myself invisible. The l thing I wanted was to be captured.

When night fell, I started looking for a safe place to hide. I came upon a deep cave that cut ri into a hill, and I knew that it would be the perfect place to stay undercover. I crawled inside a started to roll out my sleeping bag so I could finally get some rest, when suddenly I heard so rustling noises nearby.

I quickly popped on my infra-red goggles to get a better look. I was utterly shocked to see th enemy agents shuffling around a little further inside the cave! What were they doing here? I wigg back into a small hollow in the cave wall to get out of sight, then zoomed in with my goggles take a closer look at my enemies.

My heart began to pound when I realized what they were up to. They had found a dragon's n Dragon's eggs were something I had only seen in books, but I recognized them immediately. Th they were – two eggs, big and shiny and, by the look of them, almost ready to hatch. One alre had a crack running through it!

'Take 'em,' one of the enemy agents was saying. 'The boss will love this – imagine a couple trained dragons guarding our base! We can turn 'em evil and roast those Bin Weevils to bits!'

The other one cackled gleefully. 'Put 'em in the bag – don't worry about being careful, just th 'em! You know, if a dragon hatches in a bad mood it'll be more evil than ever!'

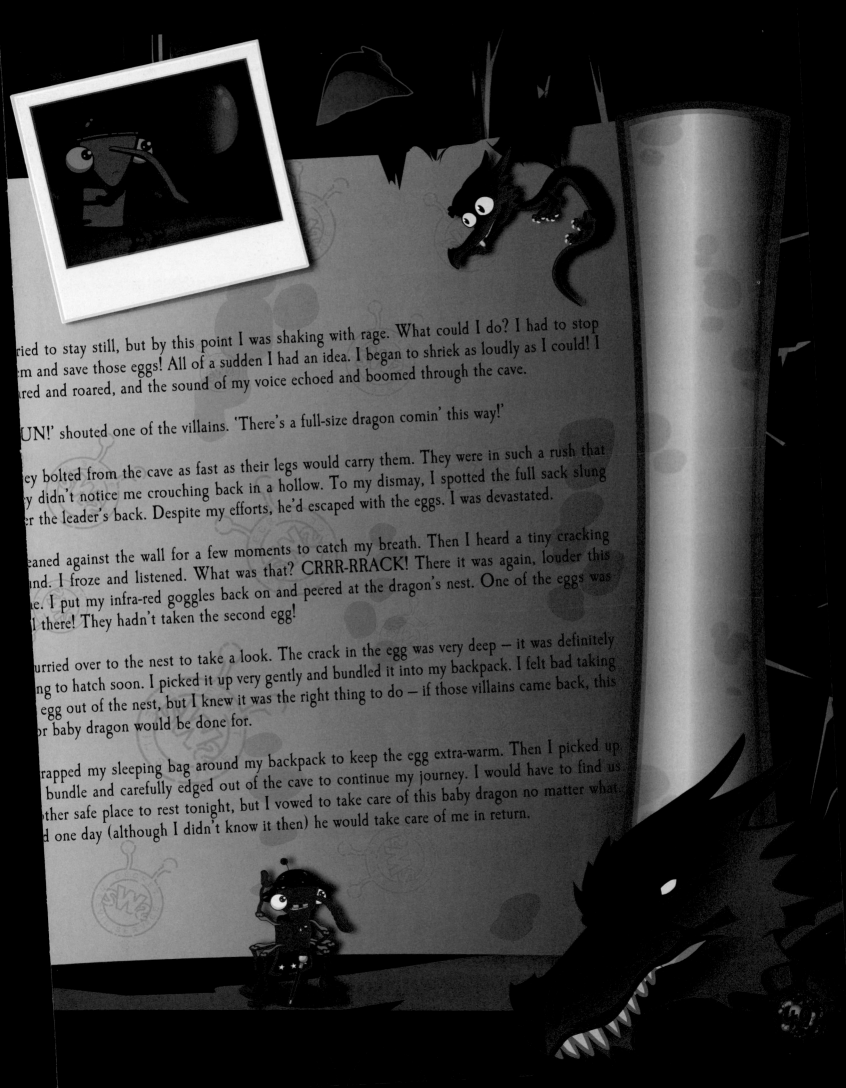

...ried to stay still, but by this point I was shaking with rage. What could I do? I had to stop ...m and save those eggs! All of a sudden I had an idea. I began to shriek as loudly as I could! I ...ared and roared, and the sound of my voice echoed and boomed through the cave.

...UN!' shouted one of the villains. 'There's a full-size dragon comin' this way!'

...ey bolted from the cave as fast as their legs would carry them. They were in such a rush that ...y didn't notice me crouching back in a hollow. To my dismay, I spotted the full sack slung ...er the leader's back. Despite my efforts, he'd escaped with the eggs. I was devastated.

...eaned against the wall for a few moments to catch my breath. Then I heard a tiny cracking ...nd. I froze and listened. What was that? CRRR-RRACK! There it was again, louder this ...e. I put my infra-red goggles back on and peered at the dragon's nest. One of the eggs was ...l there! They hadn't taken the second egg!

...urried over to the nest to take a look. The crack in the egg was very deep – it was definitely ...ng to hatch soon. I picked it up very gently and bundled it into my backpack. I felt bad taking ...egg out of the nest, but I knew it was the right thing to do – if those villains came back, this ...or baby dragon would be done for.

...rapped my sleeping bag around my backpack to keep the egg extra-warm. Then I picked up ...bundle and carefully edged out of the cave to continue my journey. I would have to find us ...ther safe place to rest tonight, but I vowed to take care of this baby dragon no matter what. ...d one day (although I didn't know it then) he would take care of me in return.

WHICH JOB COULD YOU DO IN THE BIN?

CLASSIFIEDS

Take this quiz to find out which job in the Bin is right for you!

1. What's your idea of the perfect day?
A. Bin Weevil-watching and writing notes about their weevily antics.
B. Shopping for hats and trying out new looks.
C. I'm usually busy with TOP SECRET SWS missions.

2. How would your friends describe you?
A. Gossip King/Queen.
B. Style Icon Extraordinaire.
C. Biggest Bin Brain.

3. What would you most like to achieve?
A. A prize for service to Bin journalism.
B. I'd like to open my own hat shop.
C. I'd love to catch Octeelia and rid the Bin of the threat of the WEB once and for all.

4. Where do you take your Bin Pet for walkies?
A. For a smoothie at the Smoothie Shack to catch up on the latest gossip.
B. To Tycoon Plaza to check out the new stock at Hem's Hat Shop.
C. To Castle Gam – my Bin Pet is my trusty sidekick on dangerous missions!

5. You spend most of your Mulch on:
A. Magazines and newspapers, or new ribbons for my typewriter.
B. My appearance – I have a reputation as a style icon to uphold!
C. Secret Agent accessories like shades to conceal my identity.

MOSTLY As
You could be Scribbles, the Bin's intrepid newshound!

You can sniff out a scintillating story a mile off, and you know exactly how to write it up to best effect!

MOSTLY Bs
You could be Hem, the Bin's style expert.

You set a wonderful example to your fellow Bin Weevils by looking immaculate at all times, and are always on hand to offer fashion advice to others.

MOSTLY Cs
You could be Gam, retired superhero and leader of the SW

Your first priority is the safety of the Bin, and with your skills and intelligence you make a perfect Secret Agent.

50

THE BIN WEEVIL CHANGER

The Bin Weevil Changer was created long ago by the Bin's most brilliant inventor, Slosh. The only set of plans were thought to have been destroyed, but Slosh had hidden another set! The WEB would love to get their hands on the Bin Weevil Changer, but thanks to the SWS, all their attempts have failed.

Ref No. 2547 | Level: 09
Bin Weevil Changer

ENGINE ROOM
Location: Secret Vault inside Dosh's Palace.
Purpose/Objective: To supply power and services to the Bin Weevil Changer.

1. Bio Support System
2. Status Indicator Lights
3. Body Part Distribution System
4. Information Display Panel
5. Bin Weevil Changer Pod
6. Suction Control System
7. Entrance Tube
8. Main Power Supply
9. Colour Delivery Duct
10. Hydraulic Supply Cylinder

THE BIN WEEVIL CHANGER
Location: Dosh's Palace.
Purpose/Objective: Bespoke service allowing Bin Weevils to change their appearance.

WEEVILY FRIEND MATCH

Check your star sign against your Bin Buddy's to find out what your friendship is like!

 To work out what your Bin Weevil zodiac sign is, find the golden egg you got when you joined Bin Weevils, and click on it to reveal your birthday. Then check the list of star signs on pages 54–55 to work out which sign you are. When you visit another Bin Weevil's nest you can click on their egg to find out what their birthday is, too. Once you have both star signs, cross-reference them on the friend match chart below!

Your weevily star sign

Your Buddy's weevily star sign	Aquarius	Pisces	Aries	Taurus	Gemini	Cancer	Leo	Virgo	Libra	Scorpio	Sagittarius	Capricorn
Aquarius												
Pisces												
Aries												
Taurus												
Gemini												
Cancer												
Leo												
Virgo												
Libra												
Scorpio												
Sagittarius												
Capricorn												

Why did the banana skin go to the doctor?
It wasn't peeling very well.

Just like Tink and Clott, the two of you can't go a day without getting into some kind of mischief!

 Your mutual love of partying is what brought you together. If Fling had a weevily dance crew, you'd both be in it! Dancing and music is your groovy thing.

 Eek! You're both VERY competitive – you love to keep each other on your toes, playing games and racing each other all day long at Weevil Wheels.

 You're the absolute best of friends and you tell each other everything – even that one really mega Bin secret!

 You're complete opposites, but you totally get along. Why do you think Tink and Clott are best buddies?

 You always make time for a Bin adventure together, like finding Fum, the giant that lives up in the clouds!

 You two are as close as can be! Sometimes you squabble, but you always forgive each other in the end – you can't stay mad at your bestie!

 You're always hanging out and chatting at each other's nests, and you both share a love of gardening!

 You go together like Mulch and Dosh! Nothing can come between you, not even the last delicious Dirt Donut. You'd always let your pal have it!

 Two such brainy Bin Weevils should consider going into business together – perhaps tutoring other Bin Weevils for the Daily Brain Strain. What an intellectual dream-team!

 Making and spending Mulch is your thing, and the two of you can't go a day without shopping! You think up some seriously successful Mulch-making schemes together.

 You love to make each other laugh with silly pranks and jokes – you're sure to find a hilarious buddy message when you open your mailbox!

Poetry by Ink

It's really bad.

Where is Clott's Brain?

Oh where ever is Clott's Brain?
I simply haven't got a clue,
My poor head hurts from the strain,
Pondering its current venue.
Does he keep it in a box,
Hidden under his bed?
Or wrapped in old socks,
Between two mouldy slices of bread?
Or maybe it never existed,
In any time or space,
And that is why he's persisted,
With that blank look on his face.

FAB'S FAB PREDICTIONS FOR 2013!

Well, hello there. I'm Fab, the most fabulous Bin Weevil in the Bin. I've used my cosmic powers to predict your fortunes for 2013, so pay attention while I reveal what the next year holds for youuuuu . . .

Aries (Mar 21-Apr 19)
This year you'll make even more Bin Buddies – it's that charismatic personality of yours! The party and nest invitations will be flooding in all year long.

Taurus (Apr 20-May 20)
Could this be the year you finally win that trophy you've had your eye on? Whether it's a Best Nest, Weevil Wheels or Level Up trophy, I see glittering prizes in your future!

Gemini (May 21-Jun 20)
This year you'll have oodles of cash to spend – your nest will be the envy of your buddies and your head will be adorned with the blingiest, fanciest hats imaginable!

Cancer (Jun 21-Jul 22)
You're going to make impressive progress in your career as an SWS Agent in the coming months. Just remember to make time to do other fun stuff, too!

Leo (Jul 23-Aug 22)
I see lots of relaxing trips to Mulch Island and Tycoon Island for you this year. Enjoy, and don't forget to take pics of all the cool sights you see for your magazine!

Virgo (Aug 23-Sep 22)
It's good to reinvent yourself every now and then, and you'll have lots of fun changing your appearance this year – again and again. And again!

BIN WEEVIL CHANGER

54

Libra (Sep 23-Oct 22)
Enter as many Bin competitions as you possibly can this year – you'll have luck on your side in everything you do!

Scorpio (Oct 23-Nov 21)
Now is the time to indulge your artistic, creative side. Why not create some fantastic fan art? You might find your work displayed in Flem Manor before the year is out!

Sagittarius (Nov 22-Dec 21)
Your Daily Brain Strain test scores are going to go through the roof this year! Move over, Lab, there's a new brainbox in town!

Capricorn (Dec 22-Jan 19)
You're going to meet your favourite Bin Weevils celebrity this year! Make sure you get a picture for your nest!

Aquarius (Jan 20-Feb 18)
It's all about teamwork for you this year. You'll be super-helpful when you meet new Bin Weevils who need Bin advice, and you'll be everybody's favourite supportive friend!

Pisces (Feb 19-Mar 20)
The Bin could see the arrival of a new millionaire this year! You'll make tons of cash playing games, harvesting your garden and completing missions. And then you'll have lots of fun spending it all!

What do you get if you cross an apple with a Christmas tree?
A pineapple.

BEST-KEPT SECRETS IN THE BIN

Pssst! Want to know a secret? The Bin is teeming with hidden mysteries . . . if you know where to look!

We've discovered something fishy on Mulch Island! Head over to the beach and click the beach umbrellas in sequence to see what happens. Your secret code sequence is: ORANGE, PURPLE, GREEN, BLUE, GREEN, ORANGE.

TOP SECRET: MULCH ISLAND BEACH

The Garden Inspector's plants love opera, but Mulch Island's plants love ballet! Stand on one of these rocks in the Mulch Island Jungle, perform three spins (use the 'spin' move from your actions menu) and see what happens!

TOP SECRET: MULCH ISLAND JUNGLE

TOP SECRET: EDITOR'S OFFICE

What time is it? It's secret time! Sit behind the desk in the Editor's Office at Flem Manor, then click on all four clocks from right to left to see what happens!

TOP SECRET: SMOOTHIE SHACK

Boogie down at the Jam Stand on Tycoon Island, then head over to the Smoothie Shack! Sit on all the seats in the Jam Stand and then the Smoothie Shack and see what happens. Don't forget the seat behind the smoothie bar!

TOP SECRET: SHOPPING MALL

Ever wondered what's behind that 'ON AIR' door in the Shopping Mall? Do the secret knock to open the door! Click on the three bricks around the door in this sequence: LEFT, RIGHT, TOP, RIGHT, LEFT, RIGHT, TOP.

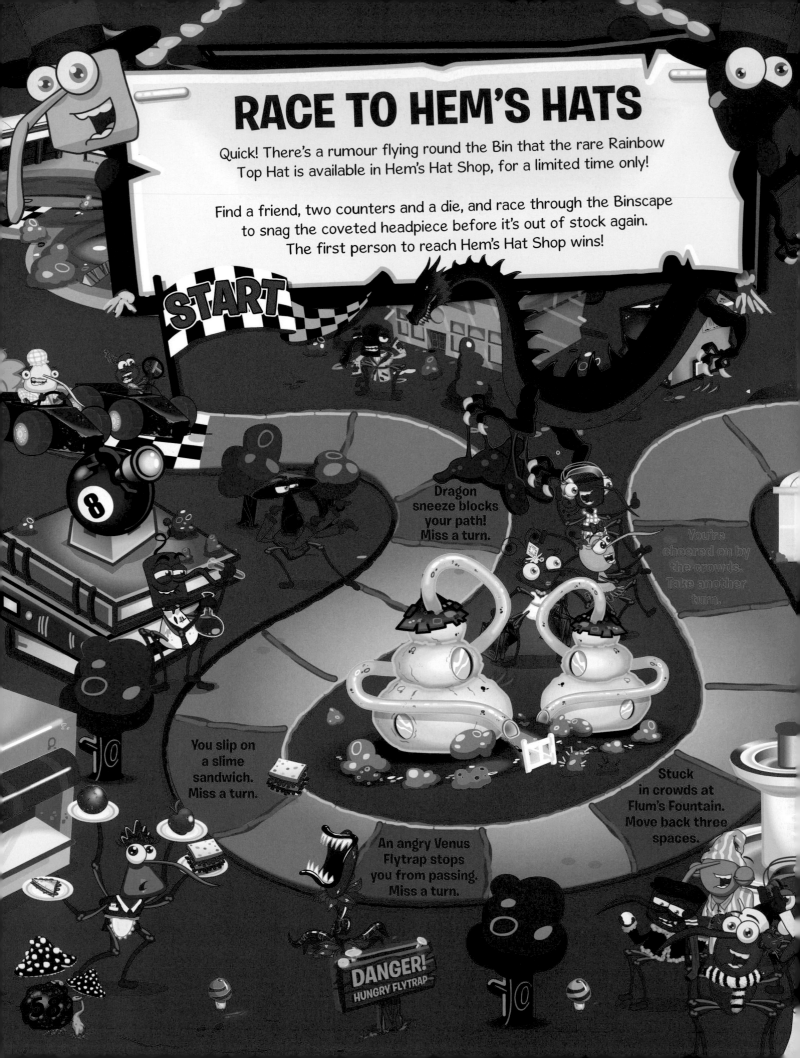

RACE TO HEM'S HATS

Quick! There's a rumour flying round the Bin that the rare Rainbow Top Hat is available in Hem's Hat Shop, for a limited time only!

Find a friend, two counters and a die, and race through the Binscape to snag the coveted headpiece before it's out of stock again. The first person to reach Hem's Hat Shop wins!

START

Dragon sneeze blocks your path! Miss a turn.

You're cheered on by the crowds. Take another turn.

You slip on a slime sandwich. Miss a turn.

Stuck in crowds at Flum's Fountain. Move back three spaces.

An angry Venus Flytrap stops you from passing. Miss a turn.

DANGER! HUNGRY FLYTRAP

Low on food.
Go back to the
beginning.

Hitch a ride
in Tink's wheel-
barrow. Take
another turn.

Gam
knows a
shortcut. Follow
him across
the bridge.

Perform
super power jump.
Move forward two
spaces.

You slip on
slime. Go back
to the start!

You fall
down the pit
of mystery.
Go back to
the start.

Eat a Bin
Burger for
energy. Take
another
turn.

Gong
gives you
a rousing pep talk.
Move forward
a space.

DOSH'S PALACE

HEM'S
HATS

ANSWERS

Page 24-25: DRAGON PUZZLES

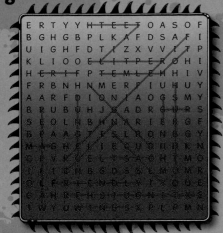

Toothbrush Puzzle:
- A is 15 Mulch
- B is 10 Mulch
- C is 12 Mulch
- D is 8 Mulch
- E is 5 Mulch

Odd one out:

Page 26: CELEBRITY SNAPS

1 = Bing

2 = Gong

3 = Bunty

4 = Figg

5 = The Nest Inspector

6 = Gam

Page 27: OCTEELIA'S WEB

Page 46-47: GLORIOUS GARDEN SEARCH-AND-FIND

Page 28-29: SPECIAL OPS TRAINING

Bin Knowledge Quiz:
1=F, 2=F, 3=T, 4=F

Sudoku:

4	3	2	1
1	2	3	4
3	4	1	2
2	1	4	3

3	2	4	1
1	4	2	3
4	3	1	2
2	1	3	4

3	2	4	1
4	1	3	2
2	3	1	4
1	4	2	3

Odd one out:

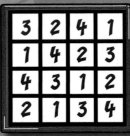

Complete the sequence:

Page 30: CRACK THE CODE

The message reads:

WE STRIKE CASTLE GAM TONIGHT!

Page 31: SWS SPOT THE DIFFERENCE

Page 32-33: HANDBAG MIX-UP

 B D H I J

 A C E F G

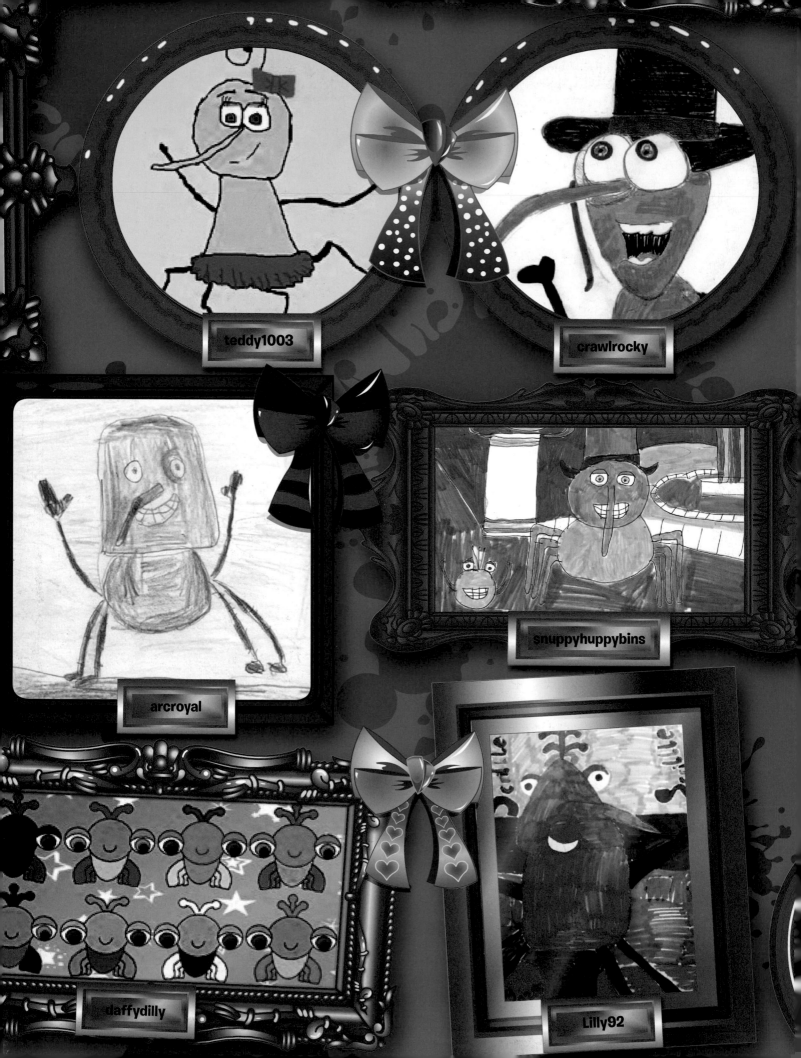

teddy1003

crawlrocky

arcroyal

snuppyhuppybins

daffydilly

Lilly92